The Moving Business Blueprint

Starting a Profitable and Efficient Moving Company

Table of Contents

Chapter 1. Introduction

Dive right into the immensely rewarding world of the moving industry with our Special Report: "The Moving Business Blueprint: Starting a Profitable and Efficient Moving Company!" Discover how simple it can be to kick-start your own successful venture, with comprehensive guidelines, effective strategies, and insider tips all packed into this exciting report. No matter if you're new to the moving business or are looking to revamp your existing setup, this report will serve as a dedicated navigator to fuel your journey towards a profitable business. It's time to 'move' mountains in the moving business - your blueprint to success awaits. Get ready to find your dream blueprint translated into actionable steps, right within the pages of this must-have guide. With infectious enthusiasm and empowering knowledge, let this be your launchpad into a thriving entrepreneurial journey. Who knew starting a successful moving company could be this straightforward and engaging? So, let's get moving! Order the Special Report now. Buckle up, because a successful moving business is right around the corner!

Chapter 2. Understanding the Moving Industry Landscape

In the business world, thorough understanding of your chosen industry is crucial; without such knowledge, it would be akin to venturing into a dense forest without a map. The moving industry is a vast and varied landscape, filled with various opportunities and challenges. This chapter will take you through the various key aspects that you need to understand, to effectively maneuver in this domain.

2.1. The Size of the Moving Industry

The moving industry is rather large, worth in excess of $18 billion in the USA alone. The industry is composed of roughly 7000 companies, operating at varying scales - from one-truck owner-operators to national franchises and international brands. This sheer size and diversity make for a competitive industry whereby companies continually innovate to stay ahead. This dynamic landscape presents immense opportunities for those who can seize them effectively.

2.2. Market Segmentation

Before jumping in, it's crucial to comprehend the different market segments within the moving industry. Broadly, the market can be segmented into residential and commercial clients.

Residential Movers These constitute the largest portion of the market. Individuals and families moving from one home to another are a constant source of business. These moves can be local (within the same city), intrastate (within the same state), or interstate (across states).

Commercial Movers This involves the relocation of corporations or businesses. Commercial moves require specialized equipment and skills, including the disassembly and reassembly of office equipment, furniture, and fixtures. But, the rewards are usually far higher, given the size and complexity of these moves.

It's important to decide which market segment you plan to cater to, as this will inform your business strategy in terms of marketing, pricing, and service offerings.

2.3. Industry Trends

In addition to the market landscape and segmentation, keeping an eye on industry trends is crucial for survival and steady growth.

Trend Towards Eco-Friendliness Many moving companies are adopting green practices, such as reusable packing materials, biodiesel trucks, and electronic paperwork. The trend is not just environmentally ethical but is also popular with clients, especially among urban and younger ones.

Technology Adoption Moving companies are leveraging technology to boost efficiency. Online booking, virtual surveys for estimates, and real-time tracking are becoming the norm rather than the novelty. Adopting such technologies sets your business apart and enhances the customer experience.

Flexible Storage Solutions In a rapidly urbanizing world, storage solutions are a growing allied service. Many movers offer storage facilities for customers in between moves or those who need to declutter. Offering such services can diversify your revenue streams.

2.4. Regulatory Landscape

The moving industry isn't just about the physical act of moving goods. It's heavily regulated and requires adherence to numerous laws, especially if your business crosses state lines.

Interstate Moves Interstate movers must register with the Federal Motor Carrier Safety Administration (FMCSA) and abide by their regulations. These requirements include offering liability coverage for goods, providing a written estimate before the move, and providing a booklet titled "Your Rights and Responsibilities When You Move."

Local and Intrastate Moves Regulations for local and intrastate moves vary by state, and even by city. You'll need to understand and comply with these local regulations.

Having a solid grasp of the regulatory landscape is an integral part of running a successful moving company, and non-compliance can lead to hefty fines, legal issues, and lasting reputational damage.

To truly understand and succeed in the moving industry, one must be familiar with its scope, market segments, trends, and regulatory aspects. This exploratory journey may seem challenging initially, but gainful rewards await those who are well-prepared and focused. It's a landscape that blends traditional customer service with ever-evolving technology and trends, creating an industry that's dynamic, diverse, and undeniably fascinating.

Chapter 3. The Essentials of Starting a Moving Company

Every successful venture begins with the essentials, and a moving company is no different. Grasping the basics will set you on the right path, ensuring a solid foundation is laid for a profitable and efficient moving company. Let's now dive into the essentials that you need to know for your new moving company endeavor.

3.1. The Business Model

The business model of a moving company primarily revolves around providing services to individuals or businesses that need to relocate. These services typically include packing items, loading them onto a moving truck, transporting items to a new location, unloading the items, and, in some cases, unpacking them.

A moving company's revenue typically depends on the number of jobs it's able to secure, how far the moves are, and on the specific additional services provided (like packing, storage, etc.). Some companies offer relocating services locally, while others cater to long-distance moves or even international relocations. Selecting your niche in this diverse industry is key to shaping your business model.

To distinguish your moving company from the competition, consider adding value-added services. For example, offering packing materials or storage options can be a lucrative addition to your business model. Think outside the box to serve a wider range of customer needs and secure a strong position in the market.

3.2. Licensing and Insurance Requirements

To operate a moving company, you need to fulfill certain legal and insurance requirements. Most countries require moving businesses to have a certain level of licensing and insurance. It protects the company and its clients against potential damage or loss of property during transit. In the United States, for instance, moving companies must hold a United States Department of Transportation (USDOT) number.

Insurance is essential too, covering liability for damages and worker's compensation in the event an employee gets injured on the job. Professional liability insurance might also be necessary if you offer packing and other added services. Consulting an insurance expert can help you understand how much and what type of coverage you'll need.

3.3. Purchasing the Necessary Equipment

Of course, a moving company cannot function without the appropriate equipment. The fundamental requirement is a vehicle to transport items. You might start with one, but as your business expands, investing in a fleet of moving trucks may become necessary.

In addition, dollies, moving pads, and straps are necessary for moving heavier items. Don't forget about packing supplies too, such as boxes, tape, and bubble wrap. As your company grows, additional equipment like GPS devices for trucks, storage units, and packing tables may be beneficial.

3.4. Hiring and Training Staff

As the demand for your services increases, you'll need to hire staff to meet customer demand. Hiring reliable and hard-working individuals who maintain a professional demeanor is crucial for the success of your business.

Offering proper training is equally vital. Training should not only involve safe and effective handling of objects but also excellent customer service. Remember, your staff is the face of your business and how they treat customers makes a lasting impression.

3.5. Building a Strong Brand

Successful moving companies owe a lot of their success to their well-established branding. This doesn't only include a catchy name and logo but also showcases how your services are unique and superior compared to your competitors. Using your brand, tell your story and project a trustworthy image to your customers. Engage in effective marketing strategies and maintain a strong digital presence to reach an even wider audience.

3.6. Setting Up Pricing Strategies

Contrary to what many believe, pricing isn't just about covering costs and making a profit. A well-developed pricing strategy can be a tool to establish a clear market position. Pay attention to what your competitors charge and ensure your prices are competitive while factoring in your costs and desired profit margins.

Remember, the more value-added services you can deliver, the more pricing flexibility you'll have. Offering basic moving services along with premium ones can cater to a wider demographic, promoting both volume of business and higher profit margins on specialized services.

3.7. Conclusion

The journey of starting a successful moving company goes beyond just buying a truck and hiring workers. It involves rigorous planning, strategic decision-making, and consistent efforts. By focusing on the essentials outlined above, you can build the groundwork necessary for a thriving, successful moving business. Always remember, success doesn't come overnight, but with determination and upholding a commitment to service excellence, your moving company has the potential to 'move' mountains in the industry.

Chapter 4. Mastering the Legalities and Registration Process

Navigating the landscape of legalities and starting a moving business is not a daunting task, given you have the right knowledge and an understanding guide at your disposal. As the saying goes, 'knowledge is power.' It is with this power that one can master the idiosyncrasies of the legal system.

Chapter 5. Choosing the Right Business Structure

First things first. You must decide on the business structure your moving company will utilize. Typically, you can choose among the following four structures: sole proprietorship, partnership, Limited Liability Company (LLC), and corporation.

Sole Proprietorship is the easiest business structure to form as it simply links the business to the owner. The key advantage is the uncomplicated tax system as any profits made from the business go to the owner's individual tax return. The drawback, however, is that the owner is personally liable for business debts and legal action.

A **Partnership** can function either as a general or limited association. In a general partnership, profits, liabilities, and management duties are divided equally, unless there is a written agreement that states otherwise. A limited partnership has both general and limited partners with the latter enjoying the limitation of personal liability.

A **Limited Liability Company (LLC)** provides more flexibility. Owners of an LLC are referred to as members, who can be individuals, corporations, or even other LLCs. This structure limits the personal liability of members, but still allows the profits and losses to be passed through to the members' personal tax returns.

Then there are **Corporations**, which are far more complex and expensive to organize but provide the most robust protection against personal liability. However, double taxation is a limitation; the corporation is taxed on its earnings and then shareholders are also taxed on the dividends they receive.

Chapter 6. Registering the Business

Once you've decided on your business structure, you need to register your new business. This involves choosing and registering your business name, obtaining tax IDs, and filing the necessary paperwork with the appropriate state agency.

Your business name is not only a significant part of your brand but is also needed for almost all business paperwork and documentation. Ensure that the name is unique and not in use by another company. In some states, a business name must also include the structure, like 'LLC' or 'Inc.'.

After your name is secured, apply for an Employer Identification Number (EIN) from the Internal Revenue Service (IRS). You can apply for your EIN online at the IRS website. You may also need to register for state and local taxes depending on where you're operating your business.

Chapter 7. Acquiring the Necessary Licenses and Permits

Once your paperwork is filed, and your business is registered, you'll need to acquire the necessary licenses and permits. The requirements may vary according to state, but all interstate movers must be licensed by the US Department of Transportation.

To obtain this crucial USDOT Number, you'll need to fill in a form known as the MCS-150, which can be done online. Once obtained, this USDOT number has to be displayed prominently on every vehicle in your fleet.

7.1. Processing Additional Permits

Apart from your USDOT number, if your business involves interstate operations, you should obtain a Motor Carrier (MC) Number from the Federal Motor Carrier Safety Administration (FMCSA).

MC numbers are specifically for businesses which transport regulated commodities across state lines, or arrange for their transport. Considering a moving service will likely fit these criteria, an MC number remains vital.

To acquire an MC Number, you need to fill the OP1 Application through the FMCSA portal. It takes about 20-25 days to obtain this number, so plan this into your startup timeline.

Chapter 8. Understanding Insurance Requirements

Insurance is another aspect of the legalities that cannot be ignored. At a minimum, your moving company will require liability and cargo insurance to cover the goods being moved and general liability insurance to cover any accidents that may occur during the job. The FMCSA requires a minimum of $750,000 in liability insurance for movers.

It is also necessary to offer customers Full Value Protection (FVP) and Released Value Protection (RVP). In FVP, the mover is liable for the replacement value of lost or damaged goods while in RVP, the mover is liable for no more than 60 cents per pound per article.

Chapter 9. Complying with All Legal Requirements

On the legal front, the moving industry is regulated by federal, state, and local laws and regulations that you must adhere to. These include compliance with the Americans with Disabilities Act (ADA), adhering to fair labor practices and wage laws, and following truthful advertising practices. An understanding of these rules is key to the initial setup and long-term success of your moving company.

Make sure you understand all the legal obligations before launching your moving business. This may seem overwhelming initially, but with time, patience, and the correct resources, you can navigate through the legal maze. Never underestimate the importance of appropriate legal foundation—it could mean the difference between long-term success and a short-lived venture.

Chapter 10. Building an Effective Business Plan

Understanding your business' needs, scope and the way it'll function is integral in carving its path to success. An exhaustive business plan is not just necessary to guide your team's efforts, it's also essential for attracting potential investors and lenders. By outlining your business' needs, goals, strategies and financial forecasts, a business plan paves the way to fruitful achievements while effectively countering any potential roadblocks.

10.1. Step 1: Executive Summary

Even though it is written as the first section of your business plan, the executive summary is typically the last to be composed. This synopsis summarizes the entirety of your business plan, focusing on its strengths. It outlines your business' operations, mission statement, business structure, product, target market and financial highlights, all within its concise magnifying glass. Remember to keep the executive summary captivating and clear, as this is the first section potential investors and financial institutions will delve into. It must set the right stage for what follows.

10.2. Step 2: Mission Statement and Company Description

Here is where you streamline your business idea to a single sentence that encapsulates your company's purpose; this is the mission statement. A mission statement should expound your company's goals and the philosophy underlying them. Alongside the mission statement, the company description should craft a blueprint of your moving business setup. This includes your business location, the nature of your moving services, any unique features your company has over competitors, and the market needs your company plans to fulfill.

Indicate here the legal structure of your business, whether it's a partnership, corporation, sole proprietorship or LLC. A fully detailed outline of the structure of the business is a significant part of business planning.

10.3. Step 3: Market Analysis and Strategies

This section should thoroughly detail your knowledge of the moving industry. It involves details about the current state of the industry, your target demographics, and an analysis of your competitors.

- Industry Description: Detail your understanding of the moving industry. This could include the current size of the industry, recent trends, who your customer base primarily consists of (homes, businesses, students, etc).

- Target Market: Research and list down your target audience. Specify these demographics according to locality, age, income, occupation, etc.

- Competitive Analysis: This involves research about your direct and indirect competitors. Learn what services they provide, their marketing strategies, their strengths and weaknesses. Based on this analysis then, you afford your business a distinctive edge in the marketplace.

Your marketing strategies are your roadmap to gaining customers. This section describes how you plan to attract and retain customers. These might include advertising, public relations, direct marketing, web presence, etc. Additionally, you can detail your sales strategies within this section.

10.4. Step 4: Organization and Management Team

Your future investors and business partners would want to know who is responsible for running the enterprise. Include an organizational chart that shows career paths and ranks within the company. This section should detail the owners and key staff, presenting their unique qualifications that equip them to lead the venture to success.

10.5. Step 5: Services

Elucidate the services that your moving business plans to offer. These can range from residential moving, commercial moving, packing services, storage solutions, long distance moving or specialized services for delicate items. Outline these services and illustrate how they cater to the needs of your target audience.

10.6. Step 6: Marketing and Sales Strategy

This section should lay out detailed marketing and sales strategies that your moving company plans to employ for revenue generation and business expansion. Detail your pricing policy, promotional strategy, sales force, sales activities, and communication, all aimed toward acquisition and customer engagement. It could also include online marketing efforts and the intended digital presence of the company.

10.7. Step 7: Financial Projection

Financial projections are critical for attracting investors. Create an income statement, cash flow projection, and balance sheet. Furnish detailed forecasts for the next three years along with an analysis of the financial data. You could include a break-even analysis that predicts when your moving company might be able to cover all its expenses and begin to realize a profit.

10.8. Step 8: Fund Request

If you are seeking funding for your moving business, it is appropriate to highlight the amount of money you need now and the amount expected to be required in the future. Also, explain how you plan to utilize these funds.

Remember: your business plan is a living, evolving document. As your moving business matures and your market evolves, your plan should too. Despite its changing nature, your business plan should always serve as a backbone for your business projections and milestones. It would be the guiding light that illuminates the path to your successful moving company.

Chapter 11. Purchasing and Managing Your Fleet

Investing in your moving fleet is likely one of the single largest business expenses you will encounter at the beginning. Therefore, making smart choices at this stage can be crucial for the overall growth and sustainability of your enterprise.

11.1. Understanding Your Fleet Requirements

Start by assessing the demand and type of services you aim to offer. Are you focusing on residential moves within the city or looking towards long-distance and commercial moves? A residential mover within city limits may just require a fleet of medium-sized trucks, whereas long-distance and commercial moving demands a fleet of large trucks that can cover hundreds of miles in a single trip.

After determining the type of moving services, estimate the size and number of trucks you'll need. Initially, you might want to start small with a couple of trucks and then extend your fleet as you expand your business. Buy trucks that are in good condition to avoid constant maintenance.

11.2. Buying Versus Leasing

The next step is deciding whether to buy or lease your fleet. Both have their pros and cons.

Buying a truck renders it a business asset, and it's a one-time cost. It's essential to recall, however, the cost of maintenance, repairs, and insurance that are ensued with purchase. There's also the depreciation to consider – a new vehicle loses value as soon as it's bought and driven off the lot. Buying used trucks is an option, but the potential for unseen mechanical issues might erupt with a used vehicle.

Leasing, on the other hand, can mean lower upfront costs and monthly payments. This frees up more capital for other business expenses, such as marketing or personnel. It also allows you to upgrade your fleet without substantial outlays continually. Yet, at the end of the lease, you don't own anything.

Analyzing your cash flow and growth prospects can guide you while choosing between purchasing or leasing.

11.3. Fleet Maintenance

Post procurement, fleet management becomes critical. Regular maintenance is necessary to prevent service interruptions and costly repairs. Develop a preventative maintenance schedule and stick to it. This might include regular fluid checks, tire rotations, brake inspections, and engine diagnostics. Hiring a dedicated fleet maintenance manager can be beneficial if your fleet size justifies the investment.

11.4. Adequate Insurance

Insurance is an essential factor to consider. Make sure that all the vehicles in your fleet have commercial vehicle insurance. Ensure you are covered for various events like accidents, vandalism, and theft. But insurance isn't just about vehicles. Worker's compensation and insurance, along with liability insurance, are crucial.

11.5. Tracking and Management Technology

With the rise of telematics technology, you can monitor your fleet like never before. GPS tracking provides real-time data on every vehicle in your fleet, from its location and speed to idle times and fuel efficiency.

Aside from providing important logistical information, these systems have safety benefits as well. The data collected can be used to analyze driver behavior and provide feedback on areas like reckless driving or excess idling, both of which can lead to unnecessary wear and tear or increased fuel consumption.

In conclusion, managing a fleet is much more than just getting from point A to point B. It requires proactive decision-making, continual monitoring, and a commitment to preventative maintenance. However, with the proper approach, your fleet can go from a substantial expense to a strategic advantage, helping your moving business to operate efficiently and effectively.

Chapter 12. Hiring and Training the Perfect Team

Getting the right team is pivotal to setting up a successful moving company. A highly professional, well-trained staff can enhance the overall customer experience and boost your brand. It's not all about strength, it's about careful handling, effective communication, and problem management under pressure.

12.1. Your Hiring Strategy

Before you start hiring for your moving team, you'll need to establish some key criteria. Consider the nature of the job - your team will need to be physically fit, but they will also need a range of customer service skills and the ability to handle complex logistical problems. Write down a clear set of qualifications and skills, including physical fitness, problem-solving, a clean driving record, and excellent customer service skills.

Moreover, consider how many people you will initially need and what roles might be necessary. A traditional moving crew may consist of a driver, packers and loaders. As your business expands, you might need to hire more specialized roles such as customer service representatives, logistics coordinators, and marketing professionals.

12.2. The Interview Process

Having selected your criteria, you can move onto the interview process. Make sure to include practical considerations such as an applicant's ability to lift heavy objects, but also see if they are able to solve problems under pressure. Put potential hires in situations that test their decision-making skills. Are they able to strategize the appropriate way to manoeuvre a large object down a narrow staircase? How do they interact with clients under stressful situations?

Remember, technical skills can be taught, but attitude and dedication are innate. Look for candidates who are eager, ready to learn, and show the potential for growth.

12.3. Training Your Team

Once you've hired your team, training becomes your next focus. This is not just about physical training – it's a comprehensive process meant to equip your team with all the knowledge and skills they need to make your operation run smoothly. Let's break this down into a few key sections:

1. Physical Training – Ensure your team has the strength and endurance to perform the heavy lifting involved in moving. Focus also on safe and effective techniques to avoid injury.

2. Technical Training – This includes how to pack, load, and unload efficiently, as well as the safe operation of any machinery or vehicles.

3. Customer Service – Teach your team effective communication and how to manage complaints or requests from clients.

4. Policy Training – Make sure all team members understand the company's policies and are well-versed on the legalities of the moving industry.

12.4. Maintaining Quality Staff

To retain quality employees in the long-term, it's crucial to create a positive work environment. This can include providing competitive pay, acknowledging good work, offering opportunities for growth, and fostering an environment of respect and cooperation.

Another bonus of investing in your staff is that it can lead to increased customer satisfaction. A well-trained, dedicated staff will provide better service, leading to positive reviews, word-of-mouth recommendations, and ultimately, more business.

12.5. Engaging with Your Team

It's beneficial to have a culture of open communication with your team and promote an environment where ideas can be shared freely. Regularly review performance, provide constructive feedback, and give employees the opportunity to discuss their views and suggestions. Your on-the-ground team often has invaluable insights into improving operations.

12.6. Health and Safety

The nature of the moving industry comes with some health and safety concerns. Make sure your team is aware of these and that you implement necessary policies and procedures to minimize injury. Personal protection equipment (PPE) such as gloves, knee pads, and back braces can protect against injuries, and regular safety training can help prevent accidents.

In the end, running a successful moving company hinges on having a strong, dedicated team. Talent recruiting, adequate training, and ensuring high job satisfaction are critical components to this end. Foster a work environment that is conducive to professional development, physical wellbeing, and open communication, and you will have laid a solid foundation for the growth of your moving company.

Chapter 13. Demystifying the Pricing Model

The pricing model is one of the most critical and sometimes complex aspects of running a successful moving business. But don't worry - let's demystify it together!

13.1. Understanding Revenue Streams

In the moving industry, there are several ways to generate income. Here are the primary ones:

- *Moving Services:* This is the primary revenue stream for your business. You charge customers for moving their goods from one location to another. Rates can be hourly or flat-rate, based on the distance covered, weight, and type of goods being moved.

- *Packing Services:* Many customers, particularly those with busy schedules or massive quantities of items to move, prefer paying for packing services. This service also allows you to add value to your service and increase customer satisfaction.

- *Storage Services:* You can offer interim storage services for customers who might not move into their new location immediately. Storage services can provide a steady income stream, as customers pay a recurring fee until their goods are moved.

- *Moving Supplies Sales:* Sale of moving supplies like boxes, packing tape, bubble wrap, and others can significantly supplement your income.

- *Valuation Coverage and Insurance:* You can upsell extended protection plans or valuation coverage to your clients, generating additional revenue and mitigating their moving risks.

13.2. The Cost Structure

Understanding your cost structure is key to pricing your services profitably. Below are the primary expenses you will need to cover:

- *Staff Wages:* Pay for your moving crew, office staff, sales representatives, and any subcontractors.

- *Vehicle Expenses:* Expenses for fuel, maintenance, insurance, and vehicle depreciation.

- *Office Expenses:* Rent, utilities, office supplies, and overheads.

- *Equipment and Supply Costs:* Outlay for moving equipment and supplies, like hand trucks, pads, straps, and specialty equipment.

- *Advertising and Marketing Costs:* Money spent on advertising and marketing your business to attract customers.

- *Insurance and Regulatory Costs:* These include business insurance, workers' compensation insurance, and regulatory permit/license renewal fees.

- *Cost of Goods Sold:* Costs related directly to service provision, like packing materials, are part of this.

13.3. Pricing Strategies

Setting the right pricing for your services can be a challenging task. Here are a few pricing strategies you can consider:

- *Cost-Plus Pricing:* Add a markup to your total cost. Ensure markup covers all overheads, leaves something for growth and expansion, and provides profit.

- *Competitive Pricing:* Set your price around what competitors charge. Be mindful not to underprice your services excessively, leading to financial loss, nor overprice and discourage customers.

- *Value-Based Pricing:* Pricing here is based on the perceived value of your service to your customers. If you believe your service provides exceptional value, you may want to price it higher than the competition.

- *Dynamic Pricing:* In peak moving seasons, demand is high, allowing you to charge premium rates.

13.4. Quote Calculation

Creating a moving quote involves assessing various factors:

- *Distance between Locations:* The greater the distance, the higher the total moving cost.

- *Time Required:* More hours equate to higher costs for labor and vehicle operation.

- *Weight and Volume of Goods:* More items or heavier items will require more time, higher staffing levels, and possibly larger or more vehicles – all increasing costs.

- *Type of Goods:* Specialty items that require extra care or equipment to move attract additional charges.

- *Additional Services:* Any add-on services such as packing, unpacking, or storage.

13.5. Automating the Pricing Process

Investing in a quote calculator allows swift, accurate estimates for potential clients. With software, your clients can enter specific details, and receive instant, automated, and exact cost estimates anytime. It saves time for your team, provides excellent customer service, and allows more accurate job scheduling.

Remember, the pricing model isn't an isolated aspect of your business. It interacts with marketing, sales, operations, and customer service, meaning any changes you make should be considered holistically. Proper pricing can lead your moving business to steady growth and profitability. It is, indeed, no longer a mystery!

Chapter 14. Marketing Strategies for Your Moving Company

Gaining a foothold in the moving industry requires a robust marketing strategy. It's the key to enhance your brand's visibility, establish credibility, and acquire new customers. Let's delve into an assortment of marketing strategies that can propel your moving company to new heights.

14.1. Understand Your Target Market

Before crafting the marketing strategy, knowing your target market is of utmost importance. Understanding their needs, their pain points, and their expectations can enable you to create effective marketing campaigns. Start by broadening your knowledge of the demographics of your potential customers: their age range, average income, occupation, and why they might need moving services.

For example, families might need moving services because they are upgrading homes, while students might need them for moving between dorms, apartments, or back home. Businesses might be on the lookout for efficient movers because they are expanding or contracting their operations.

Armed with this information, you can create campaigns tailored towards each key demographic, allowing you to cater to their specific needs.

14.2. Build a Strong Online Presence

In the age of the internet, a business without a strong online presence is one that is invisible to a vast majority of potential clients. Here's how you can build a strong online foundation.

1. **Website:** A professional, easy-to-navigate website is the cornerstone of your online presence. Ensure your website provides all-important information like your services, contact details, and customer testimonials. It should also have functionality for users to request quotes or make bookings online.

2. **SEO:** Optimize your website for search engine results with keywords relevant to your business. This could mean using phrases like "Local moving services in XYZ" or "Affordable moving solutions in XYZ."

3. **Social Media:** Utilize social media platforms that your target market uses frequently. Post regular updates, share testimonials, and interact with your audience to build a community around your business. Engage with your audience by replying to comments, sharing stories, and answering questions.

4. **Content Marketing:** Regular blogs or videos providing tips about moving and packing, information on different services, or commonly asked questions about the moving process can help improve engagement and your search engine rankings.

5. **Online Reviews and Ratings:** Encourage satisfied customers to review your services online. This word-of-mouth marketing via online reviews and ratings can enhance your brand's credibility and attract more customers.

14.3. Networking

Networking is not just essential in the B2B segment; it also applies to moving businesses. Connect with local real estate agencies, contractors, home improvement shops, or other local businesses and find ways to collaborate. This could be in the form of business referrals, joint marketing campaigns, or cross-promotion initiatives.

Remember, the more active you are in your local community, the more you will be recognized, and the more clients you will attract.

14.4. Offer Promotions and Deals

Offering promotions or special deals during off-peak periods can attract customers who might not initially have considered using a moving service. Develop special packages catering to different demographics - for example, student-friendly pricing during the start and end of semesters, or off-peak deals for small businesses.

14.5. Outstanding Customer Service

Customer service can make or break your business. Ensure that from the first point of contact, your prospective customers receive stellar service. Train your staff in customer service skills, maintain a friendly and professional demeanor, promptly respond to inquiries, and handle issues or complaints professionally.

A happy customer is a repeat customer and is also likely to refer your services to others, thereby providing economical and effective marketing for your business.

14.6. Fleet Branding

An unmistakably branded fleet of moving trucks can serve as moving billboards for your business. Maximize this exposure by ensuring your vehicles are well-designed, clean, and carry your business name, logo, and contact information prominently.

By implementing these strategies, your moving company will not only gain visibility but will also establish a solid reputation within the industry. Remember, effective marketing is about engaging with your customers, standing out from the competition, and consistently delivering on your promise of efficient, reliable moving services.

Chapter 15. Achieving Superior Customer Service

Delivering top-notch customer service is paramount to the success of your moving business. It can make or break your reputation, directly impacting your customer retention and overall profitability. Providing superior customer service can set your business apart in a saturated moving industry.

15.1. Understanding the Basis of Superior Customer Service

Superior customer service is more than just meeting client expectations; it is about exceeding them. When clients choose your moving company, they are placing their trust in you. Their experiences, belongings, and homes are in your hands. To provide superior service, you must understand these things and aim to make their move stress-free and enjoyable.

Being transparent about costs, time frames, and insurance options are critical. Providing clear, concise information without hidden fees or surprises on moving day is essential for a meaningful customer experience. It also means handling their possessions with care, demonstrating reliability and responsibility throughout the moving process.

Above all, a superior service includes friendly, knowledgeable staff who are capable of solving problems quickly and are always willing to go the extra mile for their customers.

15.2. Staff Training for Excellent Service Delivery

The first step towards superior customer service is ensuring that all staff members - from customer service phone operators to the movers - understand the importance of providing excellent service.

Training programs should be in place to teach your team essential skills like effective communication, problem-solving, courtesy, and patience. Role-playing common customer scenarios can also be a beneficial part of the training.

Having a well-trained staff that values customer service will go a long way towards achieving superior service. However, it's also essential to have an ongoing training program to consistently reinforce these principles and introduce new customer service practices and technologies.

15.3. Effective Communication is the Key

The superiority of a moving company's customer service is often judged by how well they communicate with customers. Transparency and clarity are vital from the first contact with the customer. Every detail around costs, timings, responsibilities, and any unexpected occurrences must be communicated promptly and professionally.

During the move, frequent updates about the progress will reassure your customers. They will appreciate being notified of any delays or changes so they can adjust their plans accordingly. Remember, communication is not just about delivering messages; it's about listening and understanding the customer's needs and concerns and providing suitable solutions.

15.4. Handling Complaints Effectively

In any business, there will be occasions when things don't run smoothly. Your company's reputation is not just determined by doing things right but also how you handle things when they go wrong.

The customer must feel heard and understood in a complaint scenario. The person handling the complaint should be patient and empathetic towards the customer's situation. The complaint should be addressed promptly, a resolution identified quickly, and any promises to fix the issue should be followed up timely.

Apologizing when necessary and learning from mistakes will show your customers that you care and are committed to providing excellent service, even when things don't go as planned.

15.5. Implementing Feedback and Continuous Improvement

Proactive solicitation and implementation of customer feedback are vital in achieving superior customer service. Regularly ask your customers how your team is doing and if there are areas where you can improve.

Survey customers post-move to garner feedback. Use their responses to identify trends, areas for improvement, and to uncover opportunities. Positive changes based on customer feedback show you value their opinions and are striving to provide them with the best possible service.

Customer service is an area where there's always room for improvement. And businesses that adapt an attitude of continuous improvement will find themselves at the front of the pack.

15.6. Rewarded Loyalty

Finally, a crucial aspect of superior customer service is recognizing customer loyalty. Implementing a loyalty program can be a great way to reward repeat customers and encourage them to recommend your services to others. This not only improves customer satisfaction but also promotes a positive company image.

In summary, providing superior customer service involves several inter-connected elements: understanding customer needs, maintaining clear and effective communication, training staff effectively, handling complaints gracefully, implementing continual improvement based on feedback, and rewarding customer loyalty. By embracing these elements, your moving business can achieve superior customer service, leaving a lasting impression on clients and paving the way for long-term success.

Chapter 16. Sustaining Growth and Ensuring Profitability

Maintaining steady growth and ensuring profitability is a critical aspect of running any moving company. Chasing after success is one thing, but replicating it consistently and strategically to guarantee a profitable venture is another. Similarly, expanding your moving business at an optimal rate with a clear focus on growth sustainability is crucial.

16.1. Building a Repeatable Business Model

One key aspect of ensuring and sustaining growth is to create a repeatable business model. This model should be simple to make, easy to understand, and efficient to implement, execute, and manage. A common mistake business owners make is creating overly complicated business models.

The perfect model for a moving company is one that can be executed and replicated by each person in the company, at varying levels, without knowledge or skill hindrance. Your focus should be on simplifying processes so that success can be achieved repeatedly by following set procedures with minimal deviation.

16.2. Effective Budget Management

Effective budget management is a fundamental way to ensure profitability within your business. By setting and sticking to your budgets, you can control your company's financial health. It involves forecasting future expenses and revenues, ensuring there's a balance between them.

Regular monitoring and evaluation of your company's financials will keep you apprised of any financial bottlenecks and offer you the chance to rectify them swiftly. Effective budget management doesn't just restrict itself to costs but also involves smart investment in tools, technology, and equipment that can enhance operational efficiency and thus, profitability.

16.3. Competitive Pricing Strategy

Formulating a competitive pricing strategy is vital in ensuring your company's growth and profitability. The moving industry is quite competitive, and prices often play a significant part in a client's decision over which company to hire.

Find the sweet spot where your prices aren't too high, driving customers away, or too low, cutting into your profits. A competitive price is one that provides a win-win scenario for both you and your customers while ensuring your services maintain a certain quality standard.

16.4. Streamlining Operations

Streamlining operations is one way to sustain growth and profitability. Evaluate your existing processes, identify pain points, and implement strategies to overcome them. The focus should be on improving efficiency, reducing waste, and boosting productivity.

Adopt newer technologies that can make processes faster and more straightforward. This could include a robust Customer Relationship Management (CRM) system, digitized inventories, or moving planning apps. However, remember to adequately train your team before incorporating new technology into everyday operations.

16.5. Skilled Workforce and Outstanding Customer Service

Customer service plays an impeccable role in retaining clients, acquiring new ones, and ensuring your company's growth. Train your workforce in basic customer service skills, including problem-solving, effective communication, and conflict management.

Having a skilled workforce will also contribute to the growth and profitability of your moving business. A competent team wouldn't just execute their tasks efficiently but would also ensure fewer damages, leading to lesser operational costs.

16.6. Building Relationships and Network

Networking and building relationships with real estate agents, storage facilities, and other related businesses improve your reach and visibility. You can even offer services like packing, storage, and cleaning in collaboration with your network partners.

16.7. Geographical Expansion

When your home base is fully established, it's time to consider geographical expansion. By expanding your services to new areas, you have an opportunity to capture new markets and increase revenue. But remember, the dynamics of each geographical location can vary. Thorough market research should precede any expansion.

16.8. Regular Performance Review

Finally, you cannot monitor growth or ensure profitability without a regular review of your company's performance. Regular evaluations provide valuable insights into what's working and what's not, allowing you to quickly adapt and make informed decisions.

Remember, sustaining growth and ensuring profitability is as much about the journey as the destination. It entails continuous learning, adapting to changes, and making informed decisions along the way. Build your business with perseverance and precision, and success will undoubtedly follow.

www.ingramcontent.com/pod-product-compliance
Lightning Source LLC
Chambersburg PA
CBHW062310290526
45794CB00006B/2746